Straight Up or On the Rocks:
The Story of the American Cocktail

MY FINE
FEATHERED
FRIEND

MY FINE
FEATHERED
FRIEND

WILLIAM GRIMES

NORTH POINT PRESS
A division of Farrar, Straus and Giroux
New York

North Point Press
A division of Farrar, Straus and Giroux
19 Union Square West, New York 10003

Grateful acknowledgment is made to *The New York Times*, in which some
of the material in this book first appeared, in an altered form.

Library of Congress Cataloging-in-Publication Data
Grimes, William.
    My fine feathered friend / William Grimes.— 1st ed.
        p.   cm.
    ISBN 0-86547-632-2 (hc. : alk. paper)
    1. Chickens—New York (State)—New York—Anecdotes.
    2. Grimes, William.   I. Title.

SF487.3 .G75 2002
636.5'09747'243—dc21

                                                        2001059096

Designed by Jonathan D. Lippincott

www.fsgbooks.com

1   3   5   7   9   10   8   6   4   2

To my mother, who raced out to get chicken feed,
and my father, who would have loved the idea
of a barnyard in the city

Ich wollt' ich wär' ein Huhn,
Ich hätt' nicht viel zu tun,
Ich legte jeden Tag ein Ei,
Und Sonntags manchmal zwei.
   —German nursery rhyme

I wish I were a hen;
I wouldn't have much to do.
I'd lay an egg most every day,
And Sundays sometimes two.

MY FINE FEATHERED FRIEND

ONE DAY in the dead of winter, I looked out my back window and saw a chicken. It was jet black with a crimson comb, and in classic barnyard fashion, it was scratching and pecking and clucking as it moved across the tiny rectangle of my lawn. It was, in every way, a normal chicken, except for one thing. It was in the middle of New York City.

I looked closer, blinked a few times, and shrugged off the apparition. Birds come and go in New York. Usually they're pigeons, not chickens, but like other birds, this one had wings and would probably use them. Or so I thought.

Night fell. Day broke. I looked out the back

One day in the dead of winter,
I looked out my back window and saw a chicken.

window and the chicken was still there, large as life. A little larger, actually. It looked content. It certainly showed no sign of wanting to move on. I sensed that this fly-by-night visitor was thinking about becoming a permanent resident. New York, the city of immigrants, was getting another one.

It was a fine-looking bird. Tired and poor, perhaps, but no wretched refuse. This chicken was huge, and it had obviously been eating well. Its black feathers shone, giving off a greenish purple iridescence in bright sunlight. Its beady brownish orange eyes had a healthy sparkle. They looked like the glass eyes on a stuffed toy animal. Its legs, thick and strong, supported it like two heavy-duty tripods. In Russian folklore, there's a witch, Baba Yaga, who lives deep in the forest. Her home is a hut that rests on chicken legs. I'd always found that description puzzling. Now I understood. Two chicken legs would be ideal for supporting a hut. These particular legs gave the chicken a lurching, confident gait. With its chest puffed out, it paced self-importantly, like a mid-level bureaucrat. As far as I could tell, it had nothing special to do, but it did nothing with a grand flourish. One moment it looked overweight, pompous, and slightly ridiculous. The next it seemed rather imposing, a dashing black figure on a mysterious mission.

It was the right bird in the wrong spot. The chicken may be a domestic creature, but it's not meant for the city, and that's exactly where this country cousin had come to roost. Astoria, my neighborhood, is just across the East River from Manhattan—only three or four subway stops from Bloomingdale's, in fact. It's a quiet, workaday sort of place, with three-story apartment buildings and small houses in two styles: square boxes covered in aluminum siding and brick "Tudor" houses with steeply pitched slate roofs. My own house is one of the square boxes, with gray siding and a narrow walkway on either side. With outspread arms, you can easily touch my house and the one next to it. There's very little about the house, or the area, that would entice a chicken. Even humans find it hard to get excited about Queens, New York's least charismatic borough. Except for Staten Island. Thank God for Staten Island.

Anyway, nothing much happens in Astoria. People go to work, then come home. They wash their cars, leave Christmas and Halloween decorations up for months on end, and spend far too much time looking for parking. Nancy, my wife, once dropped her wallet on the sidewalk. Someone returned it. When she looked inside, the money was still there. The only really shocking event that I can recall in my twenty years in Astoria is the day a deranged cabdriver walked into his bank, withdrew thirty thousand dollars in savings, and threw the bills up in the air on the sidewalk outside.

It's not quite fair to say that the neighborhood is a blank. Astoria has a history of sorts, starting with its name. Like most of Queens, it simply dozed for the two centuries after the Dutch sailed into New York Harbor. Then in 1839 a fur merchant named Stephen A. Halsey saw opportunity. Hoping to flatter John Jacob Astor, king of all fur traders, and entice him into a partnership, he asked the state legislature to change the area's name from Dutch Kills to Astoria. There's no evidence that Astor paid any attention, but wealthy New Yorkers noticed that bucolic Astoria, with its gently rolling hills, offered fine views of the East River and plenty of fresh air. They began building mansions near the water.

Look at the map, and you'll see that Queens is on Long Island. The opening of the Queensboro Bridge in 1909 and an elevated subway in 1917 touched off a half century land rush that turned that island's pristine woodlands, wetlands, and potato farms into a continuous, densely populated suburb of Manhattan. Astoria was the first stop along the way. Ordinary New Yorkers and throngs of immigrants found their way to the neighborhood, and no wonder. Although close to Manhattan, it was cheap, and it was safe. It still is. Greeks especially took a liking to the place, which has the largest Greek population in the world outside Athens. Starbucks did not arrive until a year ago, but almost any deli sells at least a half dozen varieties of olive and four styles of feta cheese. A lot of cars still have Michael Dukakis bumper stickers.

Television shows and films are shot in Astoria these days, although you'd never guess it. The work goes on in a complex of enormous windowless soundstages that might as well be data processing centers. They were built by the early motion-picture pioneers, then abandoned in the 1920s, when someone discovered that Los Angeles gets more than three hundred days of sunshine a year. The peeling relics they left behind are humming again, but stars do not go to local shops for a cup of coffee. There are no paparazzi hiding in the bushes. The glamour factor in Astoria remains, as always, quite low.

Astoria is a quiet neighborhood, in other words, but it is not rural, and hasn't been for at least a century. Nevertheless, it was in Astoria that the chicken mysteriously appeared. How? And why? Nancy and I tried to get to the bottom of the matter. Our first guess was that the chicken belonged to the people next door, Bangladeshi cabdrivers and hotel workers, who might be fattening it up for a feast. The bird spent a fair amount of time in our neighbors' yard, exploring the tall grasses, and it was obvious the Bangladeshis knew how to cook. Clouds of spicy steam would drift our way every day around lunchtime, filling the air with scents of cumin and coriander, so fragrant that even the meter reader would stop dead in his tracks and inhale deeply. The Bangladeshi hypothesis unraveled when the chicken hopped the fence and began spending nearly all its time in our yard. But if the chicken was not destined for the soup pot, what exactly was it up to? We were left scratching our heads.

In the meantime, I got used to beginning the day by peeking out the back window and checking for the chicken. It was hard to miss, a large black mass of feathers in constant motion. The chicken always gave the impression that it had been up and around for hours, getting lots done, while I loafed in bed. It was like the overeager worker who shows up an hour before everyone else, sleeves rolled up and ready for a really terrific A-plus day. I found it a little annoying, to tell the truth. No one wants to see that much productivity before the first cup of coffee.

Sometimes I'd hear the chicken before I saw it, cackling and clucking as it made its rounds, digging its powerful toes into the dirt border along the walkway. In spring the border would be filled with flowers, but now it lay fallow for the winter, and the chicken, bearing down, sent the dirt flying until the concrete walkway was punctuated with conical piles of rich earth. If the chicken did manage to turn up a grub or a worm, I never saw it. But it persevered nonetheless. Did the mere activity of looking for food give it a sense of satisfaction? Or did chickens ensure personal happiness by setting their expectations very, very low? The chicken would train a beady eye on a square inch of lawn, snatch at an invisible something with its curved ebony beak, and move on to the next inviting spot. Frustration was not in its vocabulary. Hours of fruitless pecking did not curb its zeal. When snow blanketed the backyard, it simply waited for the snow to melt. A lot of the time it simply paced back and forth, with that funny, half-stumbling chicken walk that seems like a model of inefficiency. In some ways, this daily program was a study in futility. But the chicken appeared to be as full of purpose, and as fulfilled, as Thoreau on Walden Pond. Its needs were few, its desires simple. Was there a lesson in this for me?

I studied the chicken closely. And as I studied, I felt warring emotions. I make my living as a restaurant critic. In other words, several nights a week I eat chicken. This one looked very appetizing. It brought back memories of an epic poulet de Bresse that Nancy and I encountered in Lyons, so large that it had to be delivered to the table in two installments. We attacked that chicken with knife and fork and no sense of guilt. As a card-carrying carnivore I have made peace with the idea of feasting off the animal kingdom. Like most diners, I don't see Thumper when I bite into a tender loin of rabbit wrapped in pancetta.

But in practice, I knew that I could not kill anything more sensitive than a tomato. My policy toward animals is pure hypocrisy. Once I meet them, I don't want to eat them. So this chicken was not going to be on the menu, especially as I began to come up with a theory about its origins. The most likely explanation for its appearance was that it had escaped from a live poultry market about four blocks away. It was on the run. Our hearts went out to the brave little refugee. We had to save it.

We also had to name it. Easier said than done. Well-meaning friends suggested Henny Penny, which we rejected instantly. This chicken was fat, but it wasn't fatuous. Someone proposed Vivian, which had a dark allure to it. But the longer the search continued, the less satisfying each new candidate seemed. We decided to leave things as they were. The chicken was simply the Chicken. The no-name name seemed right for a bird that came out of nowhere. Meanwhile, as the days passed, our new tenant began pacing the perimeter of the yard with a proprietary air, sizing things up with an appraising eye that said, "I've seen better, but I've seen worse."

When we bought the house, the backyard was a

wasteland of weeds, knee-high grass, and impoverished soil. Absentee owners had left the place untouched for several years. A rusting antique barber chair with a rotting leather seat sat in the middle of the yard like a hobo's throne. Only by hacking away at the underbrush did we discover a concrete walkway and brick paths. An ancient, arthritic hydrangea tree shocked us by bursting into spectacular bloom when summer arrived. Several old rosebushes, against the odds, survived. Two giant pine trees, nearly forty feet tall, stood like sentries on either side of the yard, giving shelter to multitudes of birds and squirrels. They made an impressive sight. But overall, our little patch of earth, measuring twenty-five by forty feet, was an eyesore. The only thing missing was a rusting refrigerator, or a car on blocks.

Like pioneers, we cleared the land and replenished the soil. We created an herb garden near the house and laid down vegetable patches near the old rosebushes. We reclaimed the perimeter and planted border beds of flowers and decorative shrubs. In time, the backyard flourished. It became a pocket paradise that yielded tomatoes, zucchini, cucumbers, strawberries, green beans, and bell peppers in three colors. We planted flower beds with lilies, moonflowers, daffodils, hyacinths, and irises. We set up arches and planted climbing roses. After the hydrangea was split in half by a lightning bolt, we replaced it with a little cherry tree that, after two years, produced just enough fruit for one pie.

The pine tree population, alas, declined by 50 percent only a few months after we took possession of the house. A ferocious nor'easter ripped across the area and, with one barbaric tug, pulled up one of the towering trees by its roots. The event was violent, the aftermath strangely peaceful. The tree fell to earth almost politely, landing in a perfect diagonal across the yard, the top neatly balanced against the far corner of the chain-link fence. A handyman came over the next day and reduced the mighty pine to a pile of wood chips.

The yard offered rich pickings for small animals. What we thought of as a garden, they saw as habitat. Every square inch of earth was precious in a neighborhood where improving the yard usually means covering it in concrete. Squirrels drilled holes nonstop in the lawn and in the garden, burying peanuts that seemed to come from an inexhaustible supply. At sunset, vast flocks of birds settled in the pine trees. Neighborhood cats spread the word of this promised land. Before long Nancy and I began to see furry faces peeking out from under the leathery leaves of a hosta plant. Behind the purple smoke bush, we would spy a creeping figure with whiskers at one end and a long tail at the other. In the early afternoon, feline forms could be seen sunbathing on the lawn. The cast of characters was in constant flux. As we worked the land,

we began following the ups and downs of the in-
digenous cat tribe.

By the time the Chicken arrived, the backyard
had seen generations come and go. The patriarch
was Chuggsy, named, as most of the local cats
were, by a neighbor who set out food on her back
porch. The legend of Chuggsy lives to this day. He
was an enormous black-and-white tomcat, with a
head the size of a softball and a fearsome gaze.
When Chuggsy walked, the earth shook. I once
crossed his path. He didn't run. He stood his
ground and then fixed me with a look that made
me take two nervous steps back. Female cats were
putty in Chuggsy's oversize paws. He was the Romeo
of Astoria, and when the mating season was in full
swing, sounds of love filled the air night after night.

Chuggsy's offspring were good-looking and full
of fun. One of the best was Cookie, a black-and-
white copy of Chuggsy, but half the size. Cookie
showed up whenever Nancy and I did gardening

work. She had no fear of humankind. In fact, every time I leaned over to weed, Cookie leaped onto my back. If I sat down, she jumped into my lap. She had a mysterious attraction to rubber. She was constantly finding scraps of balloon, or kitchen gloves, and dragging them across the yard. We never got to the bottom of that.

Cookie was game for anything, but her all-consuming project was hunting for sparrows. The abundant bird life in the backyard was her torment. There they were, dozens upon dozens of them, just out of reach, insolently chirping and cooing and flapping. Cookie became obsessed. She spent hours hatching schemes. At dusk she would pace and fume.

One evening inspiration struck. It suddenly dawned on Cookie that she could take the battle to the enemy. She approached the pine tree next door, threw her arms out wide, and embraced the trunk. Then, like a telephone lineman, she began shinnying her way up, higher and higher. She had the look Sylvester gets when he has Tweety dead to rights. Before long, she had reached the lower branches. She could taste victory.

Cookie tiptoed out onto a branch and swiped furiously at the nearest bird, which simply hopped up a few branches and resumed its song. Several more times she lunged, with no success. Running back and forth along the branch, she swatted this way and that. The birds flew upward and continued their evening preening. By now Cookie was beginning to take stock of her situation. She was twenty feet off the ground on a narrow, unstable branch, with no idea how to get down. She took a few cautious steps toward the far end of the branch, which drooped suddenly, nearly dashing her to the ground. No hope there. She looked earthward, envisioning one heroic leap. It was a long, long way down. She began to mew piteously.

In the end, I put a ladder against the tree,

climbed it, and coaxed Cookie into a basket, which I then lowered on a rope. After that, Cookie limited her military operations to the ground. Her days as an outdoor cat were numbered anyway. She was the "it" girl, too attractive to remain an outcast for long. A neighbor took her in, closed the doors, and Cookie was never again seen in the wild.

Cookie was only one of many cats that passed through the yard. One wound up in our house, for keeps. She was a little tortoiseshell, the only survivor of her litter, and she was having a hard time. Her mother, one of Chuggsy's many paramours, was neglectful, and Sweetzie, as we named this abused daughter, could often be heard mewing in fright, left to fend for herself. She had spirit, though. At the first sound of our back door open ing, she would scale the fence and patrol the backyard as we did our pruning and weeding. She had movie star looks and topaz eyes, perfectly round and glowing, like a lemur's. But her future as an outdoor cat looked bleak. She was scrawny, and whenever she managed to locate food, other cats pushed her aside. It was her fate, in the competition for survival, to be last in line.

One day she turned up limping badly. A bird's nest and scattered pine needles on the walkway confirmed my suspicions. Sweetzie had fallen out of the tree and broken her left front leg. This cat was not going to make it. Nancy and I adopted her, and the vet outfitted her with a bright green cast. She was one of the lucky ones. In the harsh Darwinian world she had failed to conquer, we saw a parade of cats vanish. Greystoke and Sooty Cat gave way to the devilishly handsome Butterscotch, who was replaced by Ugly Cat and later Ugly Cat Deux.

Chuggsy eventually disappeared. And into the yard, almost on cue, strolled two very large, very tough-looking toms. They were tabbies, with broad noses and yellow eyes, and almost impossible to tell apart. We named them Bruiser and Crusher. Bruiser had white paws, but that was just about the only way to distinguish him from Crusher. The two were inseparable. They ate together. They slept curled up together, as close as yin and yang, in a wicker basket we had set out on our small patio under the remaining pine tree. In cold weather they huddled together in a large igloo we bought for them. They groomed each other and wrestled until the fur flew and floated in the air in tufts. When Crusher would take it into his head to go off alone for a walk, Bruiser would wander the yard forlorn, mewing in distress until his pal came back.

With Bruiser and Crusher presenting a united front, many of the neighborhood cats took off for parts unknown. But not all. Two of Chuggsy's children stayed on. One was Midnight, a gorgeous long-haired female, as black as her name, with yellow-green eyes the color of Key limes. She loved to lounge under low, leafy plants, and when evening shadows gathered, you could just make her out, a deeper darkness within the darkness. When she blinked, her eyes flashed like neon lights.

The other survivor, Yowzer, bore the distinctive black-and-white markings of his father. His coat looked like a pinto pony's. He had an almost feminine face, with a delicate shell pink nose and two different-colored eyes. One was a pale blue, like the shallow end of a swimming pool. The other was sea green.

The sensitive face was deceiving, for it was Yowzer, skittish and shy around humans, who acted as strongman whenever a new cat tried to penetrate the backyard and gain access to the food bowls on the patio. These encounters were something to see. Yowzer would go face to face with the intruder, as Bruiser, Crusher, and Midnight stood nearby as backup. Yowzer would throw a punch or two if necessary, but usually it wasn't. There must have been something chilling about that pale blue eye. Or perhaps it was the strong, silent presence of the twins, matching packages of solid muscle. In almost every case, the interloper would slink away. Yowzer would follow, escorting it off the premises like a bouncer with an unruly customer. He was thorough about it too. It wasn't enough for the defeated cat to turn tail and hop the fence. Yowzer would hop right after it, follow it threateningly all the way across the next yard, and make sure it reached the sidewalk.

I T WAS THE CHICKEN'S JOB to merge into the backyard cat society, and this it did with surprising ease. One morning I looked out the window and saw the four cats lined up at their food bowls. There, right in the middle and eating with gusto, was the Chicken. Occasionally it would push a cat aside to get a better position. Tossing its head back and forth, it scattered pellets of food all over the patio. It was having a high old time. The cats were

*There, right in the middle
and eating with gusto, was the Chicken.*

nonplussed. "Where did this character come from?" their faces said. "Things were going along fine, and suddenly we're being shoved around by a big feathered puffball." The Chicken ignored the dirty looks. It had mastered the fine art of cutting in line. Somehow it knew what all pushy New Yorkers know: The best way to jump the queue is to act as if you've been there all along.

The cats, for their part, regarded the Chicken warily. To the extent that it was a bird, it was prey. But big prey. What to do? Yowzer especially was troubled. From time to time, he would stalk, press his stomach to the ground, swish his tail, and give every sign of going for the kill. Then he would develop second thoughts. A face-saving, halfhearted lunge would follow. The Chicken would flap its wings and half jump, half fly a few feet away. Yowzer would head off as though pressing business awaited him elsewhere. And that would be that.

The two sides quickly reached parity. Sometimes I'd look out back and see a cat chasing the Chicken across the yard. Ten minutes later I'd see the Chicken chasing a cat. When things got boring, the Chicken would sneak up on one of the cats and cackle. That always got a rise out of them. Yowzer, when the Chicken walked into his orbit, skulked away with the furtive over-the-shoulder look of a deadbeat who suddenly sees the bill collector. If the Chicken got too pushy around the food, Bruiser or Crusher might swat it on the side of the head. The Chicken did not seem to take it personally. It would back up a half step, shake its feathers, and resume eating. I liked to think the cats and the Chicken reached a plane of mutual respect, perhaps even affection.

The Chicken seemed to blend in effortlessly, establishing a daily routine in no time. It fed lustily in the morning, then scratched and dug for most of the day, settling down at the base of the pine tree for an occasional rest. At night it would fly up into the pine tree, pick out a nice branch, and sleep. It showed amazing confidence, I thought. Thrust into unfamiliar terrain, surrounded by clawed creatures whose intentions were hard to guess, it simply carried on. It seemed naturally bossy, and that helped, especially at feeding time. Being a chicken, it enjoyed group settings. I'm sure it would have preferred a flock of fellow chickens, but cats seemed to suit it well enough. It says something about New York, by the way, that no one in the neighborhood saw anything odd about having a chicken in the backyard. Yes, people noticed. But they did not pay much attention. After all, it could have been a snarling, frothing pit bull. Some New Yorkers keep pythons. You couldn't really object to a chicken.

Nancy and I meanwhile were in a lather of anxiety. We quickly realized that we knew absolutely nothing about chickens. Live ones, that is. In my line of work I have seen chickens in every imaginable form: deep-fried, fricasseed, poached, boiled, broiled, jerked Jamaican style, and coated in a luscious Albufera sauce at a Manhattan restaurant where the meals cost two hundred dollars a head. As a home cook I have carved, sliced, diced, deboned, and minced chickens. But amazingly enough, until the Chicken settled into my backyard, I had never dealt with a live one. In fact, I don't think I had ever even seen a live one, except in the back of a passing truck on the highway. My grandfather, as a kind of hobby, raised white turkeys on a farm in Dutchess County, New York. Surely he had a chicken or two, but if he did, they were eclipsed in my memory by the sight of hundreds of snow white turkeys stampeding from one end of an enormous outdoor pen to the other whenever a truck backfired. My inquiries about the birds did not get very far. All I needed to know about turkeys, the farm manager told me, could be boiled down to three words: "They're really stupid." A suburban upbringing had severed my ties to the world of farm and barnyard. I was almost on speaking terms with the jerboas, vampire bats, marmosets, and prairie dogs at the National Zoo, but the humble chicken was foreign to me. There was no getting around it: I knew a lot about the consumption side of the chicken equation and absolutely nothing about the production side. But now, in a very small way, Nancy and I were chicken farmers.

Our ignorance knew no limits. We didn't yet know whether our chicken was male or female, for one thing. It didn't crow in the morning, so female seemed a safe bet. But neither of us had ever had to answer the question. We finally resolved the gender issue—and began thinking of the Chicken as "she" rather than "it"—but this question was only one of many. Would the Chicken freeze to death out there? What do chickens eat? Do they have to live in a coop? Do they get lonely without other chickens? Do they need roosters to lay eggs?

One day I saw the Chicken writhing in what seemed like a death agony. Four cats encircled her, motionless, their faces a study in wonderment and concern. This was the end of the line, I decided. The Chicken was suffering from a fatal nerve disease. I couldn't bear to watch. Half an hour later she was fine. She had been taking a dust bath. Since time immemorial, chickens have rolled around in the dirt to rid their feathers of lice and mites. I just happened not to know this.

I racked my brain for chicken knowledge. Most of it seemed to come from old Warner Bros. cartoons and Mother Goose rhymes. Everything I knew about roosters revolved around Foghorn Leghorn. Hens, in my mind's eye, wore bonnets and sat in rocking chairs, knitting, or they gathered in groups and gossiped. I knew there used to be a famous chicken in New York's Chinatown that played ticktacktoe. For years he took on all comers and always scored a win or a draw. Not a great job, but

Four cats encircled her, motionless,
their faces a study in wonderment and concern.

better than hopping on a hot plate, like the "danc-ing" chickens familiar at American fairs. Dancing wasn't their only form of artistic expression, either. I recalled that years ago, when I was hitchhiking out west, a carnival family picked me up in the Nevada mountains. They were hauling a trailer, and in the trailer, they explained, were piano-playing chickens. For some reason, we never ex-plored this any further. I knew that chickens are easy to hypnotize. Al Gore, on the campaign trail, often recalled happy days in Tennessee when he would line up chickens on the back porch and put them into a trance.

My plans for the Chicken did not involve games, music, or hypnosis, though. As a first step, all I wanted to know was what to feed her. The ground outside was frozen hard, and it was pathetic to watch the Chicken hop here and there, pecking hopefully. She seemed more likely to get a throb-bing headache than a worm. The dead plants would give up a few desiccated seeds, but not enough to sustain a big, fat bird. The dry cat food I bought in twenty-five-pound bags from Costco was an obvious hit, but should I indulge this strange taste? Cats are cats; birds are birds. The food might be too rich for her blood or nutritionally out of whack. It might be like giving a small child a steady diet of Slim Jims.

A colleague put me in touch with a real-life farmer in New Jersey. He poured balm over my city slicker worries. "Chickens will eat just about any-thing," he said. "They'll eat vegetables. They'll even eat grass." I didn't need to worry too much about the cold either. "They just fluff their feathers," the farmer said. A chicken coop, I learned, is aimed at protecting the birds from predators. If there are no predators, there's really no need for a coop, although chickens appreciate a roof over their heads and a nice round perch. Winter does pose one threat. If it's cold enough, a chicken's comb can become frostbit-ten, and even fall off. There is a remedy. You rub the comb with snow and then smear it with Vaseline.

Chickens, in fact, can withstand frozen everything. In a widely reported story, a Maine woman lost a chicken in a blizzard and found it, a day later, frozen solid with its legs sticking straight in the air. She brought it back to her kitchen, intending to put it in a box and bury it, when she noticed a faint pulse in its throat. She administered CPR, including mouth-to-beak resuscitation. The chicken came around, and after being warmed with a hot-water bottle, it made a full recovery.

I felt the first glimmerings of hope. Chickens were beginning to sound like the ideal pet. Not a lot of personality, perhaps, but undemanding. Why doesn't everyone in New York have one? I thought.

THERE CAME A DAY when the Chicken made a nest. She picked a spot at the base of the pine tree and made a shapely depression in the carpet of pine needles. In her idle moments, she would plop down on her bed, cluck softly, fluff her feathers, and settle in for a long period of rest and reflection. In the afternoons, if I looked out the window, I'd see Bruiser and Crusher snoozing in the basket, Yowzer draped along a nearby wooden bench, and the dark, shapeless form of Midnight filling out the sagging seat of an old sea grass chair we had bought for a couple of dollars at a yard sale. And in the midst of the group, perfectly content, sat the Chicken. It was a heartwarming sight. We were halfway to having the only barnyard in Queens.

If Nancy and I had thought about the meaning of the nest for two seconds, we might have guessed what lay in store. Winter was giving way to early spring, and the days were lengthening. One afternoon Nancy went out to survey the backyard and take stock of the gardening chores that lay ahead. She saw something strange, a smooth, ovoid shape on the patio. An egg. Her eye traced a path to the nest. There, in the hollow beneath the pine tree, three more eggs were clustered. Nancy initially thought I had put the eggs there as a practical joke. But on closer inspection she saw that they didn't look like the local product. They were small, with a color somewhere between ecru and beige. This was it, the blessed event. Along with the herbs, the tomatoes, and the zucchini, we could look forward to fresh eggs.

Just how good were they? To find out, I organized a competition. I put our eggs to the test against two top-rated organic free-range eggs. One brand boasted that its eggs came from hens raised in "a free-roaming environment." The other claimed that its chickens were fed natural ingredients without antibiotics or hormones and that, further, the eggs were hand-gathered from "free-running" hens. When does roaming accelerate into running? I wondered. My eggs did not qualify as organic, exactly, but my chicken both roamed and ran. I pre-

This was it, the blessed event.

pared the eggs two ways: hard-boiled and fried in a little butter. The first brand, dark brown and preciously packaged in a tricky double-layer carton of clear plastic, had a café au lait shell and a pale yellow yolk. The other brand's were either white or a shade of brown varying from pale beige to mahogany with speckles. The rival eggs were enormous compared with mine, which had a thick shell and a bright yellow-orange yolk that took up nearly three-quarters of the egg. It stood tall against the white, a shimmering orb of perfect protein.

The Chicken carried the day. The gradations of egg flavor are very subtle, so freshness can easily tilt the balance. And when it comes to freshness, well, the competition was over before it began. The yolks of the commercial eggs turned slightly dry and mealy with cooking, while mine stayed fluffy and moist. The whites had not a hint of rubberiness. No contest.

The Chicken, with spring advancing, warmed to

her task. She began laying eggs at the rate of almost one a day, although some were factory rejects. One egg was quail-size. Technically, it was a peewee, the smallest of the six U.S. weight classes. Another had a strange squiggle on top, like the swirl on soft ice cream. Apparently, when chickens build up excess calcium, this happens. The brown color had nothing to do with diet or the color of the hen. Strangely enough, egg color depends on the origin of the chicken and the color of its earlobes. Mediterranean breeds with white earlobes lay white eggs. English, American, and Asian breeds with red earlobes lay brown eggs. One oddball, the Araucana, also known as the Easter Egg chicken, lays green or blue eggs.

On balance, the Chicken was a consistent, high-quality producer, and I discovered that I could help. Feeding the Chicken chopped kale, chard, or parsley would make the yolks even more orange. Adding crushed oystershells to her diet would keep her well supplied with calcium, essential for maintaining the strong bones that make for thick-shelled eggs. (To create shells, which are calcium carbonate, chickens draw on the calcium in their bones.) If crushed oystershells were hard to find, I could use crushed eggshells. The trick here was to bake the shells in the oven first. Otherwise, I was told, the Chicken might develop a taste for eggshell and begin pecking her own eggs. The idea shocked me, but I learned that hens have a mixed record as mothers. Some are attentive, rotating their hatching eggs three times a day by gently nudging them with their beaks to ensure proper development of the chicks. They precisely regulate the egg temperature by sitting for most of the day and then taking breaks that allow the eggs to cool down a bit. But some hens get bored with sitting on eggs for the three-week gestation period and simply wander off. Others clumsily crush the eggs. Mine seemed to have good technique, although with no rooster around, her motherly instincts would not be likely to get a test.

WE WERE NOW the proud owners of a healthy, egg-laying chicken. But what kind? I turned to a popular catalog put out by the Murray McMurray Hatchery ("Your Poultry Headquarters for the Millennium") and began browsing. The pages were filled with the showiest chickens I'd ever seen. There were Silver Laced Wyandottes, Golden Laced Cochins, Rhode Island Reds, Buff Silkies, Crevecoeurs, Mottled Houdans, Sicilian Buttercups, and Egyptian Fayoumis. The profusion of colors and the feather forms were mind-boggling. The Silver Laced Wyandotte, each silver feather tipped in black, has the precise, ordered speckling of a pointillist painting. Sultans, an all-white breed from southeastern Europe, come with two hairstyles, one for each sex, and both ridiculous. The rooster has a huge, cartoonish mane, parted in the middle, that falls all the way to its shoulders, while the hen has a perfectly round bubble coif that looks hair-sprayed. Buff Orpingtons, an English breed, glow regally with feathers of pure gold.

On page 15, in a section devoted to "heavy breeds," I found my chicken. It was a Black Australorp. The odd name reflects the bird's origins. It descends from the Black Orpington breed, developed in Orpington, Kent, by William Cook, who crossed a Minorca cock with a black Langshan hen, then mated the black offspring of the two with black Plymouth Rocks. The idea was to combine the egg-laying qualities of the Minorca with the heavy weight of a Plymouth Rock, all in one beauteous coal black package. The results were successful. Black Orpingtons, first exhibited in 1886, tasted good, weighed a lot, did a good job of laying eggs, and, as a bonus, had pleasant personalities. They were strong and healthy, too. Cook, who had started out with white Orpingtons, went on to develop Buff, Spangled, and Jubilee Orpingtons. All of them made their way to the United States around the turn of the century.

Then Australian breeders got into the act. The English Orpingtons, over time, had developed into a loose-feathered show bird—a "feather duster," as one dissatisfied breeder put it. Not only were they becoming less efficient as commercial birds, but their loose feathers made them ill suited to the hot Australian climate. The Australians got to work. They crossed their Orpingtons with Australian Langshans, producing a tighter-feathered, somewhat lighter breed that could lay eggs with the best of them. This mild-mannered superchicken, exported to Britain and the United States between 1920 and 1930, was called the Australian Utility Orpington, then the Austral Orpington, and eventually the Australorp. The Black Australorp soon astounded the world. One hen set a world record that still stands: 364 eggs in 365 days. I could not have been happier with the Chicken's pedigree.

IT WAS NICE to know that the Chicken could eat anything, but I still didn't feel right about the cat food. I started looking for advice on the ideal diet, but in New York, it turned out, chicken knowledge is hard to come by. The bird specialist at one Petco recommended wild birdseed. The expert at another branch said, "We have birdseed for specific kinds of bird, but because the chicken is not a specific bird, we don't have any specific food." That stopped me cold. It's specifically a chicken, I wanted to say. I ended up buying a bag of Technicolor parrot food. Its tropical flavors did not please the Chicken. Finally, I did what any adult male would do in a crisis. I called my mother.

It was the right call. Over the years, in a house filled with six children, my mother had put up with dogs, cats, hamsters, guinea pigs, and box turtles. She cared for parakeets that terrorized visitors by swooping down and perching on their eyeglasses. I vaguely recall a toad named Snavely and a fully functioning ant farm. For one tension-filled week, my mother tried to revive a wounded squirrel named Nutty Joe, carrying him in the pocket of her housecoat and feeding him milk from an eyedropper. Nutty Joe didn't make it, but my mother knew how to act in a pet crisis. She drove to the local feed store in La Porte, Texas, picked up a twenty-five-pound bag of Cargill scratch grains (a blend of milo, corn, and oats), and began shipping the grain in installments. This was more like it. Even I knew that chickens are meant to eat chicken feed.

I made a feeder for the Chicken by cutting a hole in a plastic milk jug and stapling it to the base of the pine tree. I taped over the edges of the hole so the Chicken wouldn't behead herself when bobbing for the feed. Although still keen on cat food, the Chicken seemed to appreciate the change in diet. I certainly preferred seeing her eat grain, especially after the evening when I set out a treat for the cats—leftover shreds of chicken from the stockpot—and watched in horror as the Chicken happily joined in.

My impression, from watching farmers in movies, was that chickens come running when you scatter the feed. Not so. At least, not this one, which ran joyfully when the cat food hit the bowls but regarded chicken feed as a between-meals snack. In any case, she preferred to wander throughout the day, digging here, pecking there, and only occasionally stumbling on clusters of feed. In restaurant terms, the Chicken preferred a grazing menu, or the tapas approach.

As it turns out, chickens will eat just about anything short of plastic lawn furniture. They adore leafy green vegetables. They'll peck cantaloupe rinds right down to the webbing. When the ground is soft, they hunt for worms, grubs, and insects. (One nineteenth-century manual on poultry farming that I read recommended ship biscuits, especially wormy ones.) Grains of course are welcome in any form. The Bangladeshis next door suggested cooked rice—I never tried this—and oatmeal and bran are sure to get a warm response. Corn is good, but in small amounts. Its relatively high fat content can turn a pleasingly plump bird into an obese one, thereby endangering its health and ending any chance at a career on the catwalk. ("A fat show bird is no more pleasing than a fat fashion model" is the way one poultry guide puts it, cruelly.) Wheat kernels go down well, though, and so do cooked potatoes, sweet potatoes, raw or cooked squash, and pumpkin, especially the seeds. Chickens do not mind stale bread, but potatoes, unless cut up, present a conceptual challenge: chickens tend to mistake them for rocks. Which is not to say they won't eat rocks, if they're the right size. In fact, chickens must eat rocks. Since hens don't have teeth (hence the expression "scarce as hen's teeth"), or a stomach for that matter, they need outside help to grind whole grains. Tiny pieces of stone or gravel, called grit, are added to the feed and settle in the gizzard, where the food that passes from the crop, a pouch at the base of the neck, is ground fine. One nineteenth-century poultry manual recommended pulverized crockery or pounded brick for high-quality grit.

It was almost a relief to find that some foods were not meant for chickens. A friendly correspondent gave me a list of banned substances that included avocado, chocolate, onion, raw potato, caffeine, and alcohol. That last one was a puzzler. "Do they think we're going to give the Chicken a martini?" Nancy asked.

As the days passed, the Chicken gained confidence. So did we. Initially, when I walked into the backyard, she ran away at top speed, squawking in protest. If I drew closer, she flapped over the fence and retreated to the far end of the neighbors' yard. Gradually, the Chicken calmed down. One day she ran no farther than the fence. Then she made only token dashes, just enough to keep me a few feet away. With time, she learned to tolerate my presence, although petting was strictly forbidden. If I reached out to touch her, the Chicken drew herself up, flapped her wings, and scolded me. I could understand her shyness. If I had been locked up in a live poultry market, my general impression of the human race would be poor too. But usually, if I did not reach out an offending hand, the Chicken simply looked at me with a calm, inquiring eye. I was, after all, the bearer of food. As she made this connection, the look changed to something like appreciation. The ancient connection between man and fowl was being revalidated, right in New York City.

The bond goes back millennia. No one knows

when, or precisely where, *Gallus domesticus* was first tamed. The most likely theories focus on the red jungle fowl native to northeastern India, Southeast Asia, Malaysia, and China, which is almost identical to some modern bantam breeds, although the wild males have no combs, and the wild females have no wattles. The jungle fowl was domesticated around 1500 B.C. and made its way to Europe by way of Egypt. The Roman army took chickens everywhere it went.

The chicken was not domesticated for the reasons you might expect. Its primary purpose, for many centuries, was to fight other chickens in the arena. The egg was venerated as a fertility symbol, but the rooster was prized primarily as an athlete. It was not until the nineteenth century, especially after cockfighting had been banned in many European countries, that the emphasis shifted to the chicken as a source of food and as a thing of beauty.

In 1845, Cochin chickens arrived in England, soon after the port of Canton was opened to foreign trade. The chickens, sent as a present to Queen Victoria, caused a stir when they were exhibited at poultry fairs. They were enormous, and their egg-laying powers astounded the British. Magazines and newspapers carried long articles on the chickens, with detailed illustrations of the royal henhouses at Windsor, where the Cochins were soon joined by Langshans from China and Brahmas from India. Overnight, chickens became fashionable. Breeders, foreseeing European-Asian hybrids that would make them a fortune, bid top dollar for the new Asian stars. Ordinary folk wanted them for pets. Chicken mania gripped the land, and it quickly spread to the United States, where the first poultry show was held in Boston in 1849. Daniel Webster was one of the exhibitors, guaranteeing maximum press attention. Newspapers compared the rush for exotic chickens with the tulip-bulb mania of the seventeenth century. "It was one of the most remarkable phenomena of modern times," one journalist marveled, looking back from the vantage point of 1870.

Prices for rare Asian chickens reached $100, then $200, with no end in sight. Imaginative breeders passed off chickens of unknown pedigree as "Bengal Eagles," "Whang-tongs," and "Quittaquongs," varieties that had never been heard of before, or since.

We think of chicken as an almost daily food. But in the nineteenth century it was a luxury. Chickens were primarily valued for their feathers, used to stuff pillows. Their food value was secondary. Production was limited to small farms, keeping prices high. The cost of eggs skyrocketed in winter because no one had yet discovered that egg laying is triggered by light. A hen must receive a minimum amount of light through the retina, about fourteen hours, before the pituitary gland activates the hormones in the ovary that stimulate egg laying. Artificial light will do. But in the days before electricity, even if a farmer had known that a hen needs light to lay eggs, he would not have had the technology to keep a large henhouse illuminated. Poultry farming, as a result, remained a small, seasonal business.

Champion egg layers became big news. The yearly record was always up for grabs, and special contests encouraged breeders and owners to take a crack at it. An article in *Cackle and Crow*, an old poultry magazine, lovingly recalled the first chicken to break the 300-egg barrier. The year was 1914, the place was Philadelphia, and the contender was a white Leghorn named Lady Eglantine, a resident of Eglantine Farms on Maryland's Eastern Shore. At a time when the average hen laid 70 eggs a year, she produced 314 eggs in one year, shattering the existing world record of 286 eggs, set the year before by a Columbian Plymouth Rock named

Columbian Queen. Lady Eglantine, like a champion racehorse, soon became a prized breeding commodity, earning the title of "the $100,000 hen." A victory parade was held in her honor, with a motorcycle escort en route to a reception at the Hotel Walton. The next day she was transported to New York by private railway car and received by the mayor, who presented her with a diamond-studded gold leg band. A year later Lady Eglantine died, and her owner had her stuffed.

The poultry mania expressed itself in two ways. Commercial breeders wanted to improve meat and egg production. But others simply wanted to develop the fanciest, most extravagant-looking chickens on earth. Poultry societies organized poultry shows, and the most prestigious of them all, the American Poultry Association, developed a detailed list of desirable characteristics for each breed, collected in the *American Standard of Perfection*. All this attention did wonders for the chicken's image.

"Did you know that many of our largest industrial-ists get personal delight out of a flock of chickens?" asked one poultry guide in 1944. Hollywood's most romantic stars personally attended to their flocks, it insisted, and a highly coveted poultry prize was sponsored by "one of New York's best-known play-boys."

New ornamental breeds outdid one another for striking color effects, strange hairdos, and bizarre combs. The McMurray catalog did not include, for example, the long-tailed Yokohama, a white chicken with tail feathers up to fifteen feet long. The breeds known as frizzles have feathers that are twisted and turned forward, making the chickens look as though they have been fluff-dried. The Appenzeller Spitzhauben, orange with black dots, has a dense, vertical tuft of fine black feathers on its head that looks like a tall crew cut. The Hamburg sports a brilliant red comb that looks exactly like a chunk of coral. Even stranger chickens have been reported on. Ulisse Aldrovandi, a sixteenth-century Italian scholar and chicken fancier, described Asian chickens "clothed with hair like that of a black cat," and white chickens covered in wool instead of feathers. My Australorp, I have to say, looked conservative and dignified by comparison with these trendsetters.

One journalist described the Australorp as looking like a round square. But finer eyes developed a list of visual standards, according to which points were awarded at competitions. I put my chicken to the test. The skull should be rounded at the back, the comb fine-textured and carried erect and evenly. Check. The wattles should be medium-size and rounded at the bottom. Check. The neck should be long and fine, and the legs short, strong, rounded, and set well apart. Check and double check. The eyes and plumage presented a few problems if I had any thoughts of putting the Chicken on the runway. The ideal Australorp eye, lovingly described by one poultry journalist as "full, bright, and intelligent," should be black with a dark brown or black iris. The Chicken's was limpid but unmistakably orange-brown, enough to disqualify her. Also, the feathers, although soft but not too fluffy, as required, had a purplish rather than purely green sheen. The Chicken was beautiful to us, but no supermodel. It was probably just as well. Show chickens have to pose, and I had no intention of schooling my high-spirited, willful chicken in the arts of seduction.

I looked at the Chicken endlessly, and I wondered. What lay behind the veil of animal secrecy? Did she have a personality, for one thing? Historically, this question has perplexed many minds. Our ancestors seemed to assign hens either a great deal of character or none at all. As literary subjects they have made a poor showing, compared with cats, mice, and birds. Chicken Little sticks in the mind as a negative role model, and the very annoying

Little Red Hen is a moral lesson, not a character. Henny Penny is nothing more than a rhyming name, like Turkey Lurkey and the rest of that unimpressive crew. The enigmatic black hen that "laid eggs for gentlemen" is actually one of the more memorable chickens in print, proof that the talent pool is very shallow. I browsed through the library catalog and was not tempted by *Le Poulet de Broadway*, the French tale of a dancing chicken who makes it all the way from a Broadway arcade to Hollywood. And that looked like the best of the lot.

If the hen made a poor muse, it inspired no end of superstitions. It was thought that witches used empty eggshells as boats, sailing out onto the open ocean and raising storms. As a precaution, simple folk would pierce the bottom of the shell before discarding it. Alchemists could use eggs to create tiny humans, or homunculi, by stirring secret ingredients into the yolk and then placing the mixture on a manure pile. Mixing hen's feathers with goose feathers in a pillow would cause restlessness and insomnia. Black hens, like black cats, were regarded very warily. Peasants would sometimes slip a coin underneath a setting black hen, hoping to buy its goodwill and prevent the hatching of witchlets. In popular lore, it was a black hen that delivered the money from the devil to the hapless mortal who sold his soul. It was not uncommon for black chickens to be put on trial for witchcraft and burned at the stake. Cocks and hens, as symbols of maleness and femaleness, even played a role in enforcing human gender codes. A hen that crowed aroused deep hatred and was often killed instantly. "A whistling girl and a crowing hen," the saying ran, "always come to some bad end."

No hen ever seemed less like a witch than ours. There was nothing sinister about her. But she did have an air of mystery. I was intrigued. What made her tick? I began studying the Chicken's habits and facial expressions, such as they were. The Chicken

But now she was nose to nose
with a huge, feathered ball of rage.

certainly had a strong sense of territory and firm views on personal space. That much I knew already, and Sweetzie found it out the hard way. One morning I heard a commotion outside, a squawk-fest that started at medium volume, then grew louder and more insistent. The Chicken was obviously on high alert, but why? I raced outside and saw Sweetzie, frozen in her tracks with one paw lifted like a hunting dog on point, face to face with the Chicken. I had left a basement window open, and Sweetzie, who still yearned for the great outdoors, had squeezed through the metal bars and discovered a big surprise. The backyard jungle had unleashed terror in many forms on this poor cat. But now she was nose to nose with a huge, feathered ball of rage. The Chicken, in full fury, was giving Sweetzie a hellacious tongue-lashing. In chicken language, this was a gushing torrent of four-letter words. Sweetzie reversed course and dashed for the basement window. Halfway through the metal bars, her plump rear end got stuck. There is only one thing worse than facing down an angry chicken, and that's having your helpless derriere exposed to it. With one last, desperate twist, Sweetzie extricated herself like a stuck cork, and fled to the safety of the basement.

Along with its aggressive streak, the Chicken also seemed to have an appetite for play. Was it pure coincidence that she liked to sneak up on Yowzer, the cat most likely to develop a nervous twitch when caught unawares? Time after time I saw the Chicken trot up delicately when Yowzer had his back turned, squawk a couple of times, and then watch as the cat leaped a couple of vertical feet. The Chicken, after a successful ambush, would run off jauntily, with a cackle that sounded suspiciously like a chuckle.

The Chicken was a hard read. One day I saw her perched on the iron bars outside a basement window. She sat motionless, staring hard at the glass. I watched and waited for her to move. She didn't. The performance was baffling. Was she taking inventory of the objects in the basement tool room? Or was she staring deep into her own reflection? Perhaps she had hypnotized herself. I might have to write Al Gore about this. Finally, as the minutes dragged on, and the Chicken remained paralyzed on her perch, I thought of another possibility: Her feet had frozen to the metal bar. Alarmed, I reached out a hand, and the Chicken came to life. She flapped her wings, gave me a few warning squawks, and ran off to the middle of the yard.

In the old days, when rural Americans spent a lot of time around chickens, they made a real study of their poultry. I ran across a funny article by a man who had grown up on a farm in western New York in the 1850s, tending to a flock of a hundred chickens, which he and his brother would observe, and experiment on, hour after hour. Chickens were in a way their television. Every one of those hundred chickens had a name and a distinct character, it seems. They possessed all the human emotions and character traits, in somewhat simplified form. They could be vain, sneaky, and courageous. They could be embarrassed. They schemed and plotted, especially about food. A hen that managed to catch a mouse (this talent was news to me) would saunter off to a remote location with her prize. On the way, she would make a point of giving off noises that signaled to the rest of the flock that nothing special was going on. Once out of sight, she would feast greedily.

The writer and his brother turned a cowardly chicken into a mighty David by an ingenious trick. Every time its main tormenter, a huge rooster, came near, they would throw a tidbit of food that caused the rooster to turn its back. In time the fearful chicken became convinced that it was intimidating the rooster. It gained courage. Before long, illusion became reality. The ninety-pound weakling would arrogantly kick sand in the face of the barnyard boss.

Personality in animals is a funny thing anyway. I suspect that if you studied an anthill long enough, and hard enough, distinctive traits would begin to emerge. Even ants must have their share of goof-balls, class clowns, bullies, and natural leaders. More followers than leaders, of course, but still, Napoleonic ambition surely rises to the surface once in a while. We're talking about a population of trillions.

The point is, animals can surprise you. The Chicken, for example, showed real character the night that horror descended from the sky. She had already proved herself indifferent to bitter cold and heavy snow. But on that one occasion she displayed genuine courage. It was a peaceful evening, and Nancy and I were watching television. Suddenly, what sounded like a traffic helicopter began circling overhead. These things happen. Jam-ups at the Queens–Midtown Tunnel or the Queensboro Bridge draw the choppers that transmit minute-by-minute updates to several AM radio stations. But the *thunka-thunka* sound of copter blades came closer and closer, so loud it seemed as if the helicopter was right outside.

It was. A police helicopter, searchlight blazing, was descending over my backyard. For a wild moment I wondered if it was intending to land, but it hovered just above the pine tree, searching house to house for something or someone. It was a scene straight out of *Cops*. I looked for a fleeing figure pursued by slavering police dogs, but the searchlight showed nothing more sinister than backyard barbecues and swing sets. And then my mind turned to the Chicken, roosting in the tree.

The helicopter hovered, and the downdraft from the blades set our pine tree swaying violently. The wind blew with hurricane force. It turned over the wooden bench on the patio, flipped the cat igloo upside down, and smashed heavy ceramic cat bowls. Somewhere, deep in the branches, the Chicken was holding on for dear life. I couldn't be-

gin to imagine what was going through her tiny
mind. By now, I figured, she had either suffered a
fatal heart attack or had been dashed to the
ground. But no. The next morning, amid wreckage
out of *Apocalypse Now*, the Chicken reappeared,
brimful of vim and vigor. I looked at her with new
respect. She looked at me the way she always did, a
little curiously, and hopeful that food might be on
the near horizon.

UNBEKNOWNST TO THE CHICKEN, she was
about to achieve a level of fame granted to
few of her peers. I decided to write about her in the
food section of *The New York Times*. In a promi-
nently displayed story, I told of her mysterious ar-
rival, her odd habits, and her tastes in food. I
praised her eggs. The paper sent over a photographer, who arrived with a giant telephoto lens, the
kind normally used by paparazzi trying to get a shot

of nude celebrities from afar. The Chicken was wary. The whizzing and clicking of the camera spelled danger to her, and she responded with a series of brilliant evasive maneuvers. She never actually panicked. She simply made sure that at all times there was a protective bit of shrubbery, or a watering can, or a piece of lawn furniture, between her and the camera lens. The photographer stalked patiently. The Chicken gave every appearance of nonchalance, trotting here and there as though looking for a few seeds to eat, but her shiny eye registered the photographer's every movement. If he tried to narrow the distance between them by so much as an inch, the Chicken sensed it and took action. When push came to shove, she hopped the fence and made effective use of the scrub and tall grass next door. It was an impressive display. Eventually, the picture was taken, the story ran, and I was rewarded with a bonanza of new chicken information.

Everybody in the United States but me, it

seemed, had vivid childhood memories of chickens. Older readers recalled chickens of days past
and farms that had long since been turned into
shopping malls or suburban subdivisions. Even
cities like New York had had rural patches only a
couple of generations ago. Colorful chicken stories
from younger readers reminded me that there are
still huge areas of the United States where farm life
flourishes. I even heard contemporary New York
chicken stories. I was not alone after all.

In addition to practical tips on the care and
feeding of chickens, I gained new insight into the
personality question. A man from Floral Park, in
my home borough of Queens, recalled a chicken
that used to visit his mother back in the 1930s.
Floral Park, out near Belmont Racetrack, was semi-
rural in those days, so the presence of a chicken
was not unusual. But this one would show up at
the back door every morning, tap with its beak, and
then walk into the kitchen and hop up into its favorite chair. Comfortably settled, it would watch

the letter-writer's mother all day as she cooked and cleaned. When evening came, it would hop down, walk outside, and roost in a tree.

I read with interest of a flock of hens in Pennsylvania that liked to lay eggs in clay ovens. The owners maintained a perfectly orthodox coop for their hens, but one day they bought a clay oven for baking bread. It was thick ceramic, in the shape of a teardrop, and it must have looked inviting, because once the hens saw it, they did not want to lay their eggs anyplace else. Rain or shine, they would line up in front of the oven, wait their turn, and then hop in. Not even snow could stop them. Working as a team, they would clear away the blocked opening to the oven, and then resume their routine.

I was touched by the story of a lost chicken wandering the streets of SoHo in Manhattan. A pedestrian took pity on it and tossed a piece of bagel in its direction, which the chicken interpreted as an incoming missile. It dashed into the street, and under the wheels of a passing cyclist. Sudden, violent death is not unknown in New York. But this was one for the books.

One caller wanted to know if I'd like to adopt a couple of white Leghorn roosters. The rival *New York Post*, ever helpful, assigned a reporter to see if keeping a chicken in the city is legal. The answer was yes, but did I detect a note of regret in the item that ran in the paper's gossip column?

A ten-year-old girl from Connecticut entertained me with stories about the chickens at her house. It seems her brothers had brought some chicks home from school, and one thing led to another. "We have twenty-seven chickens!" she wrote, in different-colored inks. "I painted my favorite chicken's toenails and then she disappeared! But a few months after, we found a chicken corpse with painted toenails! I love chickens and I think there is no cuter animal!"

Nancy and I were beginning to think so too. The Chicken, now that she had put down roots in the backyard, deserved a better deal, and we were determined to give her one. On a trip to the Midwest, I found a feed store and bought a fifty-pound bag of chicken feed for the princely sum of eight dollars. I sealed the feed up in twenty Ziploc bags and distributed them in two suitcases, hoping against hope that the Drug Enforcement Agency would not ask me to step aside for a lengthy conversation at the airport.

After deciding that the Chicken needed a housing upgrade, I ordered a plastic nest and perch from a poultry supply site on the Internet. It was nothing fancy, just a plastic box with a fat wooden dowel (a one-inch diameter gives the ideal foothold), but this was only a starter apartment. I wasn't ready to do a full Martha Stewart. One of my newfound experts, a chicken-loving real estate agent from North Carolina, urged me to get two more chickens. "It's just as easy to take care of three as it is to take care of one, and having other chickens around would reduce stress on your hen," he said. I'm not sure he realized exactly what the layout is in New York City, but I was giving serious thought to the matter.

ONE DAY, in the middle of spring, I looked out my window. There was no Chicken in the backyard. I went out and looked around the flower beds and peered deep into the shrubbery. I looked up into the pine trees and over the fence into the neighboring yards. No Chicken.

The hours passed. Night began to fall. Flocks of birds settled into the branches of the pine trees, singing lustily in the dwindling light. Then, in nature's great dormitory, it was lights out. The birds fell silent. For the first night in months, the Chicken was not among them.

Day dawned, chill and empty. I went out to feed

The only trace of the Chicken
was a single black feather near the back door.

the cats, hoping to see the fat form of the Chicken racing across the yard, keen to shove her way into the cafeteria line. But there was nothing.

Like the parent of a runaway child, I began racking my brains, trying to recall whether there had been any change in the Chicken's behavior or appearance. But there was nothing I could put my finger on. The previous afternoon I had watched her resting comfortably in her nest beneath the pine tree. In retrospect, she seemed a little more subdued than usual. But the orange eye that regarded me was bright and lively, and the Chicken showed her usual excitement at the sound of cat food rattling in the bowls. I searched for signs of violence but did not find any. The only trace of the Chicken was a single black feather near the back door. The Chicken was definitely, profoundly missing.

Like Garbo retiring from motion pictures, the Chicken left at the height of her popularity, well on the way to becoming the most photographed, most talked-about chicken of our time. True, there's not a lot of competition in this particular arena (the San Diego Chicken does not count). But still. The Chicken was my little star. And now she was gone.

Why?

I do not have a suspicious turn of mind. But it seemed odd that a chicken that had peacefully dwelled in my backyard for more than two months disappeared only a few days after her picture appeared in my newspaper.

I resisted the thought that evil walks among us in Astoria. It was springtime. Perhaps the Chicken was looking for love. Or were the burdens of celebrity too much? By the time a photographer from the Associated Press showed up, hard on the heels of the grueling photo session with the *Times*, the Chicken may have formed a silent resolution: Starting today, I'm looking for a place where I can lay my eggs in peace. I had also learned of the behavior known as broodiness. From time to time, hens feel the need to hatch their eggs, whether they are fertilized or not. The urge is powerful. If their owners take away their eggs, they have been known to sit on rocks or golf balls. Sometimes they sneak off and create hidden nests where they can lay their eggs and sit on them to their hearts' content. Perhaps the Chicken, overcome by broodiness, had set up a secondary egg-laying operation. Or perhaps the cats were beginning to get on her nerves.

As the anxious hours crawled by, Nancy surveyed the neighborhood yards with a pair of high-powered binoculars. I put in another call to North Carolina.

Would the Chicken return? There was hope, my expert said. "Sometimes they wander off, but usually they come back in a day or two," he said. My spirits lifted. "If it gets to be four or five days, though, there's not much chance that it will return." My spirits sank.

I wandered the neighborhood, peering into yards. I decided not to post a picture and a reward.

Evil may not stalk Astoria, but avarice might have a foothold. I envisioned a line down the block, one reward seeker after another with an identical black chicken tucked under his arm.

Once I thought I heard the Chicken delivering one of her high-volume scoldings. The sound faded, and I decided it was a rusty pulley on a clothesline. As the days became weeks, hope waned.

Nancy and I went through all the psychological stages associated with a traumatic event of this kind. We engaged in self-recrimination. Had we done something wrong? Was it our fault? Self-blame turned to unfocused anger. Who would kidnap a chicken? Anger gave way to fruitless speculation. Where could a chicken possibly go? But then again, where had she come from? Why should it seem surprising that a bird that had arrived out of the blue had simply upped and left?

Nancy was distraught. "She really was a big presence in the backyard," she said glumly. I was depressed too, far more so than I could have imagined. We had grown to love the Chicken, not to mention the daily supply of eggs. The cats, for their part, adjusted quickly. In fact, just a couple of days after the Chicken turned up missing, I saw Yowzer sprawled in the nest, sleeping so soundly that I could hear little whistling sounds coming from his nostrils.

The cats could deal with the loss. The two humans were bereft. I wrote a forlorn article in the newspaper, and readers sent their condolences, some of them written on sympathy cards decorated with roses and inscribed with sentiments like "My heartfelt thoughts are with you at this time of deep sorrow." Many of them suggested that I quiz the Bangladeshis to see whether chicken had been on their menu recently. Their suspicions were unfounded. It was one of my Bangladeshi neighbors who stopped me on the street one day and asked, in a worried tone, what had happened to the Chicken. No, the Bangladeshis were off the hook.

A Vietnamese reader sent a touching e-mail, assuring me that the entire Vietnamese population of Toledo, Ohio, would include the Chicken in their prayers to their ancestors. I was surprised to learn that there was even one Vietnamese in Toledo.

I received strange phone calls. One reported a chicken sighting in Queens. A young woman told me that her boyfriend, driving on the Long Island Expressway, had spotted a big black chicken walking on a deserted bit of road leading into Calvary Cemetery in Woodside, Queens. If it was the Chicken, I was dumbfounded. Woodside is a short ride from Astoria, but in chicken terms, it was like walking from Maine to Massachusetts. Plus, the Chicken would have had to cross Queens Boulevard, a near-expressway so wide that humans are often run down before they can reach the far side. As I tried to picture the scene, a ridiculous question kept occurring to me: Why did the Chicken cross the road?

It seemed unlikely that the Chicken could have

gotten that far. But I drove over to investigate. Calvary Cemetery, I discovered, is a very large place, and as I wove in and out of its neatly laid-out sections, I could see its appeal. The cemetery is well kept, quiet, and grass-rich. Occasional stands of old oaks offer nighttime shelter. A bird wanting to get away from it all would have a hard time finding a more relaxing spot in New York.

I approached three men digging a grave. They looked at me doubtfully, as though I might be some sort of supervisor. I hesitated. How do you inquire about a runaway chicken without sounding like a maniac? I chose the direct route. "You haven't seen a black chicken around here, have you?" I asked.

"Nope, haven't seen one," the group leader said. That sounded pretty definitive. I didn't quite know how to pursue the matter.

I drove home and called the cemetery office. The mystery was quickly cleared up. A group of maintenance workers, it seemed, kept a flock of chickens near the reported sighting. It was a case of mistaken identity. "Why don't you try St. Michael's Cemetery?" the voice on the end of the phone suggested. "That's a lot nearer to Astoria than ours is." I started to explain that chickens don't naturally go to the nearest graveyard. They're not zombies. But then I thought, Maybe they do. They don't naturally go to a backyard in Queens, but this one did. And then she left.

As the days lengthened into weeks, and months, it became clear that life with the Chicken had been a colorful chapter, but it was time to turn the page. The story was at an end, at least for us. For the Chicken, who knows? Perhaps she had always looked on our backyard, and Astoria, as nothing more than one stop in a long journey whose ending, like its beginning, we can only guess at. The Chicken might even return someday. It wouldn't be the most shocking thing in the world to wake up one morning, look out the back window, and see a large feathered form bustling around the patio, scattering cat food and clucking. It could happen. At any rate, we're ready. We have the new nest and fifty pounds of chicken feed. There are a couple of extra cats these days, but I'm sure the Chicken can push them aside and get to the food. So if anyone happens to see a fat black hen, tell her this for me: There's a light in the window and a warm nest at the base of the pine tree.